Disney's

THE LION KING

SING-ALONG

WALT DISNEY RECORDS

3

INTRODUCTION

Have you ever wanted to sing a song from a favorite movie and couldn't remember the words? Songs in movies not only entertain us, but they also help set the pace and tell us more about the story. In *The Lion King Sing-Along,* we've provided the complete lyrics to all five songs, along with colorful illustrations from those exciting scenes. If you listen carefully to the music, you'll discover things that perhaps you didn't hear while you were watching the movie. For instance, in "Be Prepared," when Scar is describing a warthog, do you know what instrument is played? It's a bassoon. See if you can identify other instruments in the songs and what they tell us about the mood, characters, and setting.

In all of the songs, there are many sounds made by striking, scraping, or shaking different man-made and natural percussion instruments. They are played in a regular pattern of long and short beats and create different rhythms that give the music its African feel. When the music for *The Lion King* was recorded, such simple techniques as tapping an empty water jug and hitting sticks against a music stand were sometimes used to make these sounds. You can make up your own percussion sounds using cereal boxes, pot lids, or sandpaper, and play along with the songs, if you like. But above all, we hope you enjoy the music and relive the movie as you sing along to your favorite songs.

Creative Manager: Antoinette Portis
Art Director/Designer: Eileen Powell Mooney
Assistant Designer: Kara Valeri
Illustrations: Walt Disney Feature Animation and Rick Brown
Cover Illustration: Michael Jackson

Printed in the United States of America
ISBN: 1-55723-598-8

Table of Contents

Circle of Life

From the day we arrive on the planet
And blinking, step into the sun
There's more to see than can ever be seen
More to do than can ever be done
There's far too much to take in here
More to find than can ever be found
But the sun rolling high
Through the sapphire sky
Keeps great and small on the endless round

CHORUS

It's the circle of life
And it moves us all
Through despair and hope
Through faith and love
Till we find our place
On the path unwinding
In the circle
The circle of life

(REPEAT CHORUS)

I Just Can't Wait to Be King

I'm gonna be a mighty king
So enemies beware!

Well, I've never seen a king of beasts
With quite so little hair

I'm gonna be the mane event
Like no king was before
I'm brushing up on looking down
I'm working on my roar

Thus far, a rather uninspiring thing

Oh, I just can't wait to be king!

You've rather a long way to go,
Young master, if you think...

No one saying do this
Now, when I said that I...
No one saying be there
What I meant was...
No one saying stop that
What you don't realize is...
No one saying see here
Now see here!
Free to run around all day
Well, that's definitely out...
Free to do it all my way

I think it's time that you and I
Arranged a heart to heart

Kings don't need advice
From little hornbills for a start

If this is where the monarchy is headed
Count me out
Out of service, out of Africa
I wouldn't hang about
This child is getting wildly out of wing

Oh, I just can't wait to be king!

Everybody look left
I know my...
Everybody look right
Oh, no...

Everywhere you look I'm...
Standing in the spotlight
Not yet!

Let every creature go for
broke and sing
Let's hear it in the herd
and on the wing
It's going to be King Simba's
finest fling

Oh, I just can't wait to be king!
Oh, I just can't wait to be king!
Oh, I just can't wait to be king!

Be Prepared

SPOKEN

I never thought hyenas essential
They're crude and unspeakably plain
But maybe they've a glimmer of potential
If allied to my vision and brain

SUNG

I know that your powers of retention
Are as wet as a warthog's backside
But thick as you are, pay attention
My words are a matter of pride

It's clear from your vacant expressions
The lights are not all on upstairs
But we're talking kings and successions
Even you can't be caught unawares

So prepare for a chance of a lifetime
Be prepared for sensational news
A shining new era
Is tiptoeing nearer

And where do we feature?

Just listen to teacher
I know it sounds sordid
But you'll be rewarded
When at last I am given my dues!
And injustice deliciously squared
Be prepared!

SPOKEN

Yeah. Be prepared.
We'll be prepared
...for what?

For the death of the king.

Is he sick?

No, fool!
We are going to kill him...and Simba, too.

Great idea!
Who needs a king?
No king, no king, la la la la la la

Idiots! There will be a king.

But you said...

I will be king!
Stick with me and you'll never go hungry again!

Yeah, all right!
Long live the king!

SUNG

It's great that we'll soon be connected
With a king who'll be all-time adored

Of course, quid pro quo, you're expected
To take certain duties on board
The future is littered with prizes
And though I'm the main addressee
The point I must emphasize is
You won't get a sniff out of me

So prepare for the coup of the century

Be prepared for the murkiest scam
(OOOOOOOOOO, la la la!)
Meticulous planning
(We'll have food!)
Tenacity spanning
(Lots of food)
Decades of denial
(We repeat)
Is simply why I'll
(Endless meat)
Be king undisputed
(Aaaaaaah!)
Respected, saluted
(Aaaaaaah!)
And be seen for
the wonder I am
(Aaaaaaah!)

Yes, my teeth and ambitions are bared
Be prepared!

Yes, our teeth and ambitions are bared
Be prepared!

HAKUNA MATATA

Hakuna Matata!
What a wonderful phrase
Hakuna Matata!
Ain't no passing craze

It means no worries
For the rest of your days
It's our problem-free philosophy
Hakuna Matata!

When he was a young warthog
When I was a young warthog
Very nice.
Thanks.
He found his aroma lacked a certain appeal
He could clear the savannah after ev'ry meal
I'm a sensitive soul though I seem thick-skinned
And it hurt that my friends never stood downwind

And, oh, the shame
He was ashamed.
Thoughta changin' my name
Oh, what's in a name?
And I got downhearted
How did you feel?
Ev'rytime that I...
Hey! Pumbaa! Not in front of the kids!
Oh. Sorry.

Hakuna Matata!
What a wonderful phrase
Hakuna Matata!
Ain't no passing craze

It means no worries
For the rest of your days
Yeah, sing it, kid.
It's our problem-free philosophy
Hakuna Matata!

Hakuna Matata!
Hakuna Matata!
Hakuna Matata!
Hakuna Matata!
Hakuna Matata!
Hakuna Matata!
Hakuna Matata!

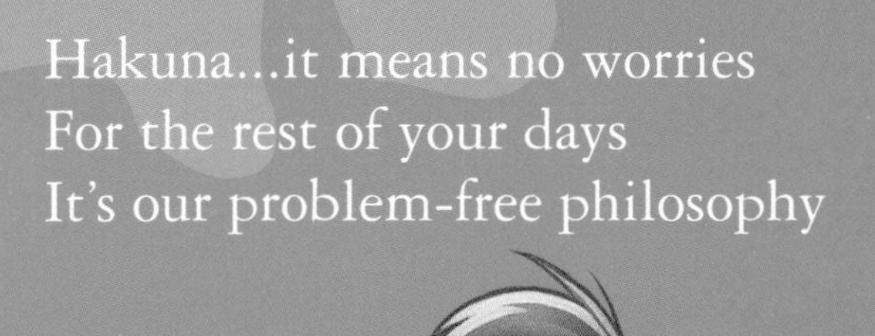

Hakuna...it means no worries
For the rest of your days
It's our problem-free philosophy

Hakuna Matata!
Hakuna Matata!
Hakuna Matata!
Hakuna Matata!
Hakuna Matata!
Hakuna Matata!
Hakuna Matata!
Hakuna Matata!
Hakuna Matata!
Hakuna Matata!
Hakuna Matata!
Hakuna Matata!

Can You Feel the Love Tonight

I can see what's happ'ning
And they don't have a clue
They'll fall in love and here's
the bottom line
Our trio's down to two

The sweet caress of twilight
There's magic everywhere
And with all this romantic
atmosphere
Disaster's in the air

CHORUS
Can you feel the love tonight?
The peace the evening brings
The world, for once, in perfect
harmony
With all its living things

So many things to tell her
But how to make her see
The truth about my past
impossible
She'd turn away from me

He's holding back, he's hiding
But what, I can't decide
Why won't he be the king
I know he is
The king I see inside?

CHORUS
Can you feel the love tonight?
The peace the evening brings
The world, for once, in perfect
harmony
With all its living things

Can you feel the love tonight?
You needn't look too far
Stealing through the night's
uncertainties
Love is where they are

And if he falls in love tonight
It can be assumed
His carefree days with us
are history
In short, our pal is doomed

The Music Behind the Movie

Music is an important part of the total movie experience. It helps support, make clear, and move the story along with the energy and mood that the director and writer imagine for each scene. When it is closely woven into the thread of the story, the movie audience sometimes doesn't even realize how strong an effect the music has on them.

The three people who create the music are the composer, lyricist, and arranger. The composer writes the music, the lyricist writes the words to the songs, and the arranger (sometimes called the orchestrator) picks the combination of instruments and voices that will be used when the music and songs are recorded. Working closely together, the composer, lyricist, and arranger discuss how they hear certain parts of the music being played. Then they meet with the director of the movie to go over instruments, tempo (how fast the music goes), and which singers will be used. The conductor, musicians, and sound engineers come in to record the music only after the composer, lyricist, and arranger have completed their jobs. It is through the talents of all these people that movie music is made.